A Fire in the Hills

A Fire in the Hills

৵

poems

Afaa M. Weaver

尉
雅
風

🐓 Red Hen Press | *Pasadena, CA*

Book layout by Rebeccah Sanhueza

Library of Congress Cataloging-in-Publication Data

Names: Weaver, Afaa M. (Afaa Michael), 1951– author.
Title: A fire in the hills: poems / Afaa M. Weaver.
Description: First Edition. | Pasadena, CA: Red Hen Press, [2023]
Identifiers: LCCN 2022026558 (print) | LCCN 2022026559 (ebook) | ISBN
    9781636280820 (hardcover) | ISBN 9781636281025 (paperback) | ISBN
    9781636280837 (ebook)
Subjects: LCGFT: Poetry.
Classification: LCC PS3573.E1794 F57 2023 (print) | LCC PS3573.E1794
    (ebook) | DDC 811/.54—dc23
LC record available at https://lccn.loc.gov/2022026558
LC ebook record available at https://lccn.loc.gov/2022026559

Publication of this book has been made possible in part through the generous
financial support of Francesca Bell.

The National Endowment for the Arts, the Los Angeles County Arts Commission,
the Ahmanson Foundation, the Dwight Stuart Youth Fund, the Max Factor Family
Foundation, the Pasadena Tournament of Roses Foundation, the Pasadena Arts &
Culture Commission and the City of Pasadena Cultural Affairs Division, the City of
Los Angeles Department of Cultural Affairs, the Audrey & Sydney Irmas Charitable
Foundation, the Meta & George Rosenberg Foundation, the Albert and Elaine Borchard
Foundation, the Adams Family Foundation, Amazon Literary Partnership, the Sam
Francis Foundation, and the Mara W. Breech Foundation partially support Red Hen
Press.

First Edition
Published by Red Hen Press
www.redhen.org

Acknowledgments

Poems in this collection have appeared in the following journals and anthologies.

5AM, Academy of American Poets, American Poetry Now, American Poetry Review, African American Review, Black Imagination, Chicory, Ibbetson Street, joINT, Jubilat, Somerville News, The Hopkins Review, The Nation, The New Yorker, and *The Pushcart Anthology.*

for
Loretta Miller

心

CONTENTS

III

Standing to America, bringing home
black gold, black ivory, black seed.

from "Middle Passage"
by Robert Hayden

A Fire in the Hills

NOTES AS OUR DEAD SEEK JUSTICE

Let another world be born . . .
—Margaret Walker

In the video, two pairs of eyes
two positions of power, all and none,

or all and then the none of losing it all
where soulless cops go when they die.

                      Say Floyd was bad anyway, prone to slip
                      around instead of going straight on ahead

                      Whose straight is it anyway? Not ours.

In the stories we tell of who we are
so who we are will always be kept
by keepers of souls, ripped flesh
of theft across generations, sunsets
planted in bloodied fields of rice,
cotton. In the stories folk relieve
themselves of outrage, one scream
at night, one at sunrise, by and by.

                      Say Floyd was not inclined to do what right
                      said to do, or what right promised if he did

                      Who IS right? Not you.

Brother, I have seen your face
in my mirror, I have seen my fear
in your eyes, I have felt your joy
in my joy, even when I do not know
the final thing that made you cry.
I know the whispers when we go
into spaces requiring a suit and tie.

Say Floyd wasn't up to some standard
of being in the world, of measuring up

Who's doing the measuring? Not us.

Black Lives Matter is truth
carved in the air we breathe.

I

IN A BORDER TOWN

In this version of the city, no one dares read,
ragtime grows underneath Washington's obelisk,
not a monument but a threat to the clouded sky.

Next door to McCormick's, a telescope sits,
looking over the harbor, inside all of what is,
for a new constellation, *the hidden dancers*,

a joining, convergences that come only when
September moons bring heavy rains, a deluge
to sound alarms to haul in the blue crabs.

In all of this we are overgrown ants, brittle
on the tongue, held up above ourselves singing
Southern chants for spells to soften the hard.

What names us? I ask a man shuffling in bags,
a man who knows the giant ants we have become,
who knows us, but says now we have no name,

but purple iris in a golden vase over the harbor,
peace wrapping itself over the city's north border,
where horses reign over the emptied corners,

where I climb back into the old way of dancing,
wiping away the spinning top hairdos with thick
masks over the need to be naked and breathless

so I can be freed from the one spent song.

ALL AMERICAN

Rickie keeps fifteen basketballs
in his mother's house, some regulation,
some filled with sand to throw as weapons,
some deflated and hung with his old shoes
over near the trophies growing decrepit,
a ball for the game he scored fifty points in,
a ball for the blocked shot he made on a boy
from the white team who was eight feet tall
with feet all crossed, long arms flailing,
a ball for the first night they all got drunk,
a ball for the night he came home nodding,
the night his mother screamed "My Lord"
when he started to lose his jump shot.
Sleeping, he watches the trophies play,
men in chrome suits defending man on man with
half-courts lit by street lamps on a playground,
out in the county traveling home on a bus,
sneaking bottles of wine when the coach naps,
standing together for the photographer,
making the all-state titles, courted by scouts—
a ball for the first prick of the skin,
a ball for the life swirling around him
a river's vortex where he is drowning,
a ball for the two children he can do nothing for,
taking salt water from his eyes to wet their tongues,
a ball for the scholarships still sitting
in his mother's dresser beside court notices,
a ball for the audiences screaming and stomping,

a ball for time and a ball for the way his
skin just clings lazily to his bones now,
the way age comes like punishment, steadily,
the days falling like heavy footsteps.

MY FIRST GUN

Not even a week out of prison he sticking
the thing in my face, six-inch barrel, twenty-two
or thirty-eight, ages I just might not make.

Minding my business is minding his
in our world, the top of the hill, high point
of the valley, Milton Avenue, our grave.

This is a world folk will name with cameras,
The Corner and later *The Wire*, sad stories
of children not yet born, our children, cherubs.

A gun changes things, changes your mind,
not even a week out of prison he sticking
the thing in my face, and I count the chambers.

Six chambers, six the sum of two times sacred three,
three the number of parts of God or a liquor bottle,
the cap, the head, the body, a shallow torso to break.

A gun changes things, changes your Black mind,
makes you want one to talk back to the one pointing
in your face, but dumb guns don't talk. They wait.

When they speak, they speak in thunder, the loud
tap on the body to demand that it open itself up,
edges of Black skin screaming, falling away.

MATH LESSON

If they shoot over there, I duck
to where the trash leads to the door
and I count to twenty-four, or till they
stop all the shooting and I can sell a cap
in the alley behind the grocery store

one bullet, two bullets, three bullets
my education gonna set me free
one bullet, two bullets, three bullets

I live on the fifth floor, fifteen steps away
from the elevator today, five steps yesterday
when Stink Face's hit man made me pay
for the caps I owed, but I ran and say
I'll talk about how his punk ass up the way

one bullet, two bullets, three bullets
my education gonna set me free
one bullet, two bullets, three bullets

I told the teacher give me my "A" or be
a statistic, and she said "you the statistic, you
little ignoramus," and when I jumped she
jumped first, told me she got a calculator
that'll make ignant little nubians disappear

one bullet, two bullets, three bullets
my education gonna set me free
one bullet, two bullets, three bullets

SHOTGUN

If the church had a been open,
                     the preacher
standing on the corner,
           the Bible in his hands,
the sun tamed down
by old ladies with eyes
         pinned down
                on the block
                         watching over us,
the block more
                      a place full of life insured
by the sound of birds,
        then it might not have
been the way it was,
            the way they were
two young men,
          —one running from the other.

If there had a been a hand
                  on a mama's hip
with a finger in the sky
shifting the stars around
to show these children
          a real power.

If the church had a been open that afternoon
                     and not the middle
of that shotgun
               broke down with fingers

not much more than a child
        loading shells,
picking it back up,
              pointing at a back
running away, running to hide, running—

If the church had a been open,
        a manchild might have lived

MY HISTORY HOMEWORK, MR. JEFF FORT

Dear Mr. Fort,
Since my teachers on strike my father
and my mother teaching me at home now.
My father told me I should tell your story
for my history homework, the story of your fight
to get dignity for Black people, the kind of dignity
that got you in trouble with the FBI. The "I" part
is what my mother said stand for idiots. I don't
believe my mother, but I don't really believe
my daddy either. I'm like *Why is Mr. Jeff Fort*
in prison anyway? But I guess I am suppose
to ask you because you the one locked up. You
been locked up for a long long time. It musta
been something really bad that you did. I mean
it must be much worse than what I saw when
I went to the school library and looked you up
on the library computer. I don't have no computer
at home. But I was looking at your picture
of when you was young and you looked so sweet.
I ain't trying to flirt Mr. Fort. I'm just a little
girl. I'm just twelve years old, but you had such
a innocent face. Well, I hope this letter make
some sense, and I hope you get it. When you
read it, please don't be sad about my writing.
My English teacher say I write too much the way
I talk, but this is for my history class. Seem like
to me English ain't got nothing to do with history,
but I am probably as wrong as I can be. I know

I'm just a little girl, just twelve years old.
My teacher like it when I use the however,
so I can say—however it be that I am so young
I want to know for my history why the bad thing
you did was so bad because you was such a sweet
young man when you was just a little boy.

BLUES IN FIVE/FOUR,
THE VIOLENCE IN CHICAGO

In movies about the end of our civilization
toys fill the broken spaces of cities, flipping over
in streets where children are all hoodlums, big kids
painting themselves in neon colors, while the women
laugh, following the men into a love of madness.

Still shots show emptiness tearing the eyes of the last
of us who grew to be old, the ones the hoodlums
prop up in shadows, throwing garbage at us,
taping open our eyes, forcing us to study the dead
in photos torn from books in burned down libraries.

Chicago used to be Sundays at Gladys' Luncheonette
where church folk came and ate collard greens and chicken
after the sermons that rolled out in Black churches, sparkling
tapestries of words from preachers' mouths, prayer books,
tongues from Tell Me, Alabama, and Walk On, Mississippi.

Now light has left us, the sun blocked out by shreds
of what history becomes when apathy shreds it,
becoming a name the bad children give themselves
as they laugh and threaten each other while we starve
for the laughter we were used to before the end came.

GAME OF LOSING, 1968

I take a toothbrush to the soles and clean
the threads so my new Stacy Adams speak
to the nonbelievers, brand-new knit pants,
my high-boy shirt collar starched, my knife
in my pocket, my roscoe under the car seat,
a hundred-dollar bill wrapped around twenties

a wife, two outside women, liquor and cards
can't nobody tell me street life ain't sweet—

Two double shifts in the coke oven, a check
fine as Wanda's eyes, rent paid up, I'm high
on the fat hog, car clean, card game at the bar,
tell Dolores *the Deacon got a prayer meeting,*
head on over to Wanda's to lay up for a week,
let the women work to make the long money

a wife, two outside women, liquor and cards
can't nobody tell me street life ain't sweet—

The coke oven so hot my sweat rolled
like the lies on a broke preacher's tongue,
rattling like always. Dreams say life just
a game of blackjack, a new deck, the dealer
showing his hands, as if he ain't cheating,
while we draw cards to burn this city down

a wife, two outside women, liquor and cards
can't nobody tell me street life ain't sweet—

THE SIRENS OF SAIGON

Fire engines, police cars, firecrackers that whistle,
sounds that poke into the night from dullness, and you
are back home in boxer shorts, no shirt, in the middle
of Federal Street with no sounds except the echoes
of sleep, slip and scratch of pieces of trash like whispers
only dogs can hear, and you see the dogs, sometimes
with no heads or with heads and nothing else, sitting
on top the bodies of men they tried to save in the heat
and the rain, and you scream out because in dreams
screams stop the injustice of the sleeping memories,
reviving things buried in places they bury heroes.

The Marine Corps takes bodies and makes weapons,
minds turned to yes machines, jumping on command
into places where there is no sanity, where they do you
the justice they call "building men" so you came home
lighter, thinner, faster, a waddling turkey become hawk,
all death, even in the stillness of eyes appearing serene
from a perch, and I wanted to go where you went,
where a man is made a man while women wait for you
to come back to them able to be what women want.

We were kids and you were brave and all muscle
when bullies attacked us at the public swimming pool,
fighting them with a combination lock, yelling backwards—
"Y'all go on, get in the pool. I got this" and I looked back
to see the flailing of arms over bodies like a black bush
blooming against slivers of light buckling in steamy heat
burning the way sun must have felt just after the rain

somewhere in the bush where you took the dead, tossed
them or what was left of them in trucks to go home.

When you went to war I wanted to follow you, follow
the trail of endings that began in beds where you passed
the hurt inside you into me, two souls aching as one.

REQUIEM FOR THE COUPE DE VILLE
a backstory for The Wire

If I can borrow that lament for a guitar and say
you took a fine time to leave me, B.B. King
won't mind that I ache that way when I see
what time has done to the cruiser that took men
away from the tightness of life in mills, on docks,
to let them roll around the block in luxury
and power, let them command the windows
with buttons and cool their own air when air
in houses had no choice, what they have done
to the long way a Cadillac took a corner, the hood
emblem like the prow of a ship parting the asphalt
to announce the kingly way we owned pavements
and alleys before the sheets of plywood covered
doorways where mothers sat with hair grease
and plaited their daughters' hair on Saturdays,
before the blank empty nothings grew in spaces
where our homes once stood, the absence now
the rubble, what time has done to the rubber mats
we brushed and scrubbed with Comet, details
summed up in what car washing has come to be,
detailing—an age where the engine and the wires
are an internet, and the steady hum of V8s comes
under the list of options in memories of big cars,
the rolling thrones of men who announced twelve-
hour shifts, missing limbs, sweat and sweet
potatoes lying upside one another as if to make
an act of love in the plate, food they paid for
in jobs that proved the miracle of a Black faith

in payment for believing in what would not
believe in them, the hard windows that planned
their lives the way men washed these cars, these
prizes for getting up inside a day that wanted
to knock them down, make them beg to live.

A POEM FOR FREDDIE GRAY, BALTIMORE

Each heart its own vessel, each wish
a summation of a day not even that heart
can know, and here now, in this moment,
this pulled out flesh of time, undone is
what it comes to be, undone to do again,
somewhere in the rolled back eyes
of repeating what we call history when
history cannot be repeated. We make
new memories each time we breathe,
and breathing fire we remove care
from the core of what we call love because
we have come to believe no one cares,
as the air is filled with meaningless bits
of meaning cut to shreds, walked on,
forgotten. If tomorrow never comes,
it is the fault of some misplaced moon
and not the failure of what we know
is human, what we know has mind and
wish and hope carved out of spaces
where we learned to live despite hatred.

WHAT A FELLOWSHIP

for Mother Emanuel AME

In these clasped hands we see the seeds
of what has come to be, the tiny Black faces
of children chained into ships headed to sea,

not an invitation to a better life, not a vote
for the human, but the deadened greed, a wish
against what life means to the living, a cruelty

above the requirements of evil, our ambition
to live, to survive, to grow beyond chains now
our only hope in row after row of bloody pews.

In these clasped hands we see the business
of selling human beings, white hands of banks,
the Black hands of enemies selling enemies

to regal promenades in France, in Belgium,
to arrogant philosophies of enlightenment,
a plodding Kant, a foolish Hume, murderers

in the name of knowledge, architects of theft,
a broad sweep to rape the world and grow fat,
to assume, to consume, to accumulate, to kill.

In these clasped hands we see the endless heart,
proud hands that bent heads down to save them,
caring souls that made a new love from carnage,

the wreckage of lives, piles of bones crumbling
to dust in mounds all around, forming breath
from stench, forming the sweet Sunday dinner

after church, after gathering around the Word
of this new God with a promise of a redeemer,
a hand with the power to end death's bondage.

In these clasped hands we hear the songs,
the mourning, the celebrations from worlds
left in Africa, forgotten except in the pulse

of what we remember of the drum, the stomp
of holy dances, of invoking the Holy Spirit
to visit, opening our prayer to wind, to fire

to the great wash of oceans, to mountains
rising and falling in visions, to dominions
over fish, fowl, beast in Eden's contract.

In these clasped hands we hear Philadelphia,
white crochet crowns on heads of our matrons
waiting to receive communion, throats clearing

for the next hymn, the ritual cheers to pastors
stuck in old sermons, the occasional Baptist
eruption in misty AME precision, the way

we wind the stairs to building a life where
the brick and mortar are the bone and soul
of courage, of the get on up now, somehow.

In these clasped hands we hold the hope
of another day, braided on strands of grief
across what divides us, what makes us one.

AN ELEGY FOR LUCILLE CLIFTON

. . . onto a heathen country . . .
—Lucille Clifton, from "slaveships"

It's the old Shirley Highway, the road
a woman inspired, flat in the curves,
the way for farmers to go home.

I turn to hear the way you reach deep
in the crevice of a tale to let me know
the secrets of how to get through.

there is a fire in the hills, are we lost?

It's my father's last new car, the green
Chevy he bought from Charlie Irish
just as I was getting to know the price.

Mill towns drop out of the lips of clouds,
the way Buffalo must have puffed
at night, and I know the legend you are.

there is a fire in the hills, are we lost?

If a radio could catch the frequency
of a magic woman with ears to heaven,
it would sit still now between us.

The words rise up from the way
we lose time in the fold of bye and bye,
the slipped anacrusis of gospels.

there is a fire in the hills, are we lost?

II

WHAT IS LEFT

In early morning after midnight, the time
of a *golden essence*, the new moon tilts
the edge of the horizon. I am full of nausea,
mac and cheese with bacon just before bed,
to bed too late to keep the circadian cycle.
The tilting jolts everything, the dogs snoring,
the cat on the bed pushing against our legs,
the in out of her paws like a baker kneading
dough for some butter biscuits. If I fall off
the edge of this bed too high above to let me
touch the floor, I will choose to be a clown
who carries a rock in his sock for the clowns
in the audience who see a Black man's strength
as some kind of joke, some thing to be taken
down and away, until we are left naked.

In our will, the blues of holding our children
when they cry for their milk as the moon tilts,
singing to them so their mothers can sleep, going
out in mornings, striding inside neighborhoods
full of sun, beauty, and fear, knowing it all falls
the way seasons come and go. The one constant
is how the world has a chokehold on dreams
we dream in skin too dark for those who fear
the dark. We walk the streets, our inheritance,
streets with sun and moon undermined
by what robs the world and thinks Black men
are the unwanted, what was not finished when
truth says we are the genius fear will not see.

THE GREAT FOOT

A great foot is Black and big,
standing square and toes up in Macy's,
without a sock on a river in New Orleans,
they call it Mississippi and the great foot
roars its head up, then its dreams slap like slush.
In the open fields of hay and alfalfa with
another foot, more feline perhaps, thin ankle
brown but with honey, ordering the set motion
of rain, pulling the sun like wool from a spindle,
the great foot is a priest, big toe and all.
What power, what ecstasy of doom in its thrust
and smash down on the earth or the glass
and steel and stomping eyes of the walking dead,
a whim, a motion forward to clean the planet.
The great foot is in a shoe on the leather,
heel up and toe pointing to the center where
earth turns to hot metal cracking under the
skin of the continents, there a dance, a melody,
a definite conk, and the words "Say it Loud".
"I'm Black and I'm Proud," said the foot.
Madness perhaps, ten dark days in the silence
of complete meals and the evening radio shows,
a woven rug and a Queen Anne chair and
"The Shadow Knows." In 1950 the foot was
aware of impending change, the sudden dip history
was dreaming of, the backward sway in rotation.
"Don't let nobody turn you round," said the foot.
"Also, I am great, I support a nation unseen,

I dance, I die, I come kicking and blood-filled,
I run in the dead small reflection of sun
in glass and there I leap."

WHAT ELIZABETH BISHOP
COULD NOT KNOW

Black women keep secrets tied up in hankies
they stuff in their bras, secrets of how their necks
are connected to their spines in the precise gyration
of a jelly sweetened in nights they had to keep
to themselves, nights prowlers came in to change
the faces of their children, secrets like the good
googa mooga laughter they do with each other
when something affirms their suspicions, when
their eyes are made the prayerbooks of fate crafted
in the wisdom that knows there is no north or south
in Black wandering, searching the new land, a song
they wrestle from Black men, the broken ones
who had to be shown where and how to stand,
how to respect pain and the way it governs itself,
secrets, things made out of generations and not kept
in the glass selections of an old jukebox.

PROPOSITION JOE, FROM THE GRAVE

The day you realize Tony Soprano's mama
is not your mama, you don't live in Dunkin' Donuts,
and you hate northern New Jersey because it is
not Philadelphia or St. Louis or anyplace other
than the grist in the air turnpike world of a television
show. It's that day you wake up healed, freed up
from another fascination with America making itself over
in the land of television, and Junior won't show up
at your door with some far-sighted hit man carrying
tweezers who forgot his eyeglasses but is intent
on putting the squeeze on you, and you stop being
over-polite to all your Italian friends as you have been
healed and realize they are actually insulted by all
of this. Think of the limitations, just pizza and cement
boots when the world is being carved and shaped
by genius. So it is, you are free and don't have to weep
for Christopher, who wants so much to make a movie
out of his life, and that is the wheel of this carnival,
one real life in the center while the rest of us spin
on its reflections on itself, each one further away
from the way a body feels when it is alive until one day
we are healed, one at a time, from the need to be alive
inside a mass of things we create in a web of circuits
and electrons and invisible forces flying from satellite
to satellite, when it makes you wanna jump up inside
yourself, Oh . . . just do it so the world will not forget
you once had real skin and breath and farted in real
time with all else that makes us more than television.

CHARLESTON

In a fountain at the harbor, children
wash themselves in water spraying
in the heat. They count themselves dark
and light. The aircraft carrier sits
in the moist nothing of salt water, tons
of tons weighing in the soft splash.
We count our wishes, to be free,
to be at ease, to be in abundance.
Above us spirits whirl in a thunderhead.

On steps across from the slave mart,
I peel an orange for the slow rip of its flesh
in my thumb, the sweet dotting of my nose
with its juice. I suck the threads of it,
gaze at the wooden doors now closed,
at the empty space inside with iron hooks.
I can see the white folks' heads checking
available cash in front of naked Africans
chained, bereaved, and listening to
a cruelty yet to be born. I can smell
the congregation of odors, humans fresh
from slave ships or working in fields, and
humans fresh from beds of fine linen,
sleeping with fingers in Bibles and prayers.

This is not a petty thing because we have
a rental car with an air conditioner, a tape
player, and various cushions. We have come

far to do this, to gaze out from the banks
of this plantation river to the rice fields,
to walk in Charleston. I keep the heat
from threatening my life, and I wonder
if I could have survived slavery to be old,
if being old is all there is to live to be.
I walk around the slave quarters and hear
African languages speaking in magnolias.

JOBS OR NOT, THE HUSTLE

for Phil Levine

In the last round before the card game, truck drivers
winding down the walkway to climb in the cab,
sleep lunchtime away, orders for subs came through,
D'Angelo with the same pencil he used to take bets
on the games, marking down who wanted cheese
and steak, who wanted the pure meat, hamburger,
with a layer of cheese on the fries like varnish,
and the bosses came to him, too, edging in for free
lunch, promising an extra minute on the half hour,
but we took what we wanted, rode down to the harbor
for clams and horseradish, or drove home to see
the wife for a quickie and a real sandwich while the kids
were out back playing, we took what we wanted,
like hunters on the prowl in the woods somewhere,
plucking fruit from some farmer's tree, taking down
what belongs to all of us.

       Work went that way some days,
the galvanized walls, chicken wire windows, cameras
hid up in the corners we all knew inch by inch, the
thin whir of ball bearings in the conveyor belts like
a whistler's song, coming home from the dryadic
with a bag full of something belonging to somebody
else, like the turkeys and hams we got at Christmas
until the basket shrunk down to the size of the holiday,
Elijah a day worker for a day labor temp agency.

All we wanted when the hour came for the orders
was to get what went with what we did, beating

sameness over an anvil of time with a hammer made
of wishes here where a sub sandwich with everything
meant dragging ourselves through a garden where
saints went to do time.

WHEN WE ARE TRUCK DRIVERS

after Tom Waits' "Big John & Phantom 309"

It's either deliver or nothing, a million miles
logged in with coffee and NoDoz on the long uphills
through West Virginia, the winding down on the other side
to where the lights say like sirens "come on in here and rest"
         where Big John
and his rescue rig can pull you back from the jackknife,
the sick V the thing makes while you try to uncurl
the CB from around your wife's arm, still sleeping
in the hollow of the last load, is it here, O Lord, where
the highway is the last stand for cowboys, the land laying
open the way it should, promises rolling on forever
when you pull up in Tulsa to fill the tank, step down
from the cab in an old pair of boots, a wallet on a chain,
grit in your hair that's familiar and friendly, and the
welcome way you stink, she smiles to know you
earned it, and she earned you, when she asks you to sing
the song you heard when you were really young and not this
not quite forty fullness of ache that comes too early
in the tally, but never mind because counting only counts
with time and the load when you back up to the dock
and tell them it's all there, the dead weight of rock salt,
or the load of dried food they pick up off the frame
and take whole, containers that stack up on freighters
as you wonder why God won't tell them you are
the guardian angels of this country, that nothing moves
if you don't wake up in the truck stop, tickle her on the arm
so you both can go wash up and get some breakfast,
call home, check on the kids, look

down on the sun crawling up to you
and pray you make the deadline, that you get back
without staying up for two nights again, hitting the rainstorms
and slick downhill runs with drivers who think
they own you, who know nothing about asking
is it here, where you hold the country together, your
hand in hers, hers around the worried slick of her own hair
over her ears that is a solemn prayer like sugar candy
that home won't be some wreck in the sky—this time.

THE N LINE TO BROOKLYN

If we invite the poor to create their own lives, they sing
in places we have called the public, their cups, their dress
from home that we call *native*, some bright colors pulled
with their hands, thread by thread, holes mended that we
will not see, only cups, hats, some things that can be
turned upside down to receive, the coins, the mean energy
of frowns under MP3 players listening to the program.
These foreigners are no longer quaint or interesting
as they name America as foreign, the palace across
the Rio Grande, shimmering promise for more than rocks
that form in the throat when there is nothing, or when dreams
seem like nothing against the place where a small chance
looks like a door blown in the side of a wall in heaven
by renegade angels, Blessed Virgins of Guadalupe setting
the laws on fire, burning the ecclesiastical greed of militia
patrolling borders in SUV luxury, elephant opulence
to those who walk from Oaxaca to this place where wealth
does not know responsibility, will not speak its names.

The train moves into a long space between avenues,
the old frames of the subway speed by, a wall it seems,
a wall outside these metal walls that could collapse
against something made of stone, and the beggar team
begins, the man in his woven cloth, his guitar come from
under a blanket, hidden there like a hunchback's hunch,
and his compadre, a woman with the upside down thing,
a hat this time, the song coming from some authentic room
where people loved to hear it at this time of day or some

other time, a place of grace, not this dissing in silent gestures,
passengers locked into the places of their own lives,
working or not working, spokes in the broken wheel
of America, or less than spokes, worn sprockets
with no ears for the lines of beggars and their music,
fingers pressed to strings, searching for a pulse.

GOOD UNCLES

Out of the same place where we first saw pig knuckles,
or the day the omniscient cousin brought a pair of nunchucks,
cracked them across his own head trying to make the things do
what Kato could do, who was really Bruce Lee and the uncle
we all wish we had, the ultimate cool man who showed you cool
the way cool sometimes came to be, world travelers on the corner,
it came out of the smartness of knowing how to jack up a car
so it would not fall on you and the flat tire or crack the chassis
in front of the cutest girl in the block or the cutest boy if you knew
you were a boy who went cool that way, it was the *un* of things,
the pardonable absence from the real, the thing that questioned
macaroni and cheese, the evening glance of light on fingers
holding cigarettes on the corner of *Good and Evil*, black hole
only the real denizens of *The Wire* know, not lookers peeping
in on roughness that names the tutelage of men in Baltimore,
or places called cities that know the spinal cord of a sailor's port,
uncles coming into town looking for what made their sex work,
bright bodies and liquor and fistfights with men who knew not
the rough way a merchant ship rolls up the side of a wave and kills
men along with what kills the wind and stars lost in galaxies,
the way the flat rolling earth comes down to the Gulf in New Orleans,
where knuckles have their own mind in the hands of men who teach
the world how to make a space for them, to lay open and wide
so they can roll their stink and sweat, wishes and fears, handmade
by sleepers in heaven who roll human beings like tobacco in paper,
the rough stockyard way a city makes flat contracts with lakes,
Chicago, the beef smell of lines drawn in concrete that names
the secret soul of the separate aggregate, gangs and gangsters,

cowboys in 1950s cities walking streets where there were no
horses or tumbleweed or cactus or dust storms or bowlegged cows
or houses made of outhouse wood like the ones down home,
and down home the naming place of all that came to be good men
who knew they had to make men, draw them up out of ignorance
down in the wells where the unproven young cling to stone
walls above the clear water in what could be a hell, draw them up
on the chain pulleys that delivered cold water to emptiness
and teach them how to be full and inviolate against the takers.

THE SHAW BROTHERS

for the Drunken Boxing Masters

If we had the space in the backyard we could have built
a Shaolin temple of our own, or at least one of the chambers,
the sun sparkling off the edge of those shiny blades,
silk outfits popping with that invisible power, iron palms,
golden shirts, eagle claws, death touches, and most of all,
flying, we would be flying, higher than after two gallons
of battery acid cheap wine, or Sunday's holiest dance,
the earth trembling when our bodies shake to ancient wisdom
when Hong Kong came to Black America and saved us
from the lack of answers in the box of riddles life came to be,
we cheered, ate popcorn or the contraband chicken taken
from the kitchen keeping place, and all else that made
Saturday kung fu the first level in Paradise, never mind Dante,
never mind the way the world turned flat at the edge
of where we lived, with the drowning river between us
and what lay all around us in a world that was round, we
had the secrets slid to us from the old connections
because Egyptian mystics sent the secrets to India and China
then back to us as we watched quadruple somersaults
ending in spinning triple twirl back kicks, masters who
melt iron and stop waterfalls, snatch dead warriors back
from six feet under, stomp their feet and make an army rise up,
just when somebody ate the Babe Ruth without sharing
and we started practicing in the movie house, reverse
punches and steel fingers, eyeball staring contests to see
who could make the building shake, throwing steel darts
we made at home out of aluminum foil that won't fly,
letting loose the secrets this time in a world of Kool-Aid,
blessed by eyes peeled to stars, touching nirvana with fingers
weaving the tapestry of what holds us together, what makes life.

RICHARD PRYOR IS DEAD

It must be Miss Rudolph the Voodoo Lady
come to collect her dues for laughter,
or the temporary effect of some ointment the CIA put
on his favorite pig foot, or the Tibetan extremists
who want the biggest ransom in the world
and are about to declare him Buddha of Hollywood so
he can get his insurance scam together and pay his bills,
some more platinum kind of reality other than us
not being able to touch him anymore.

ALL GHOSTS RISE, BLACK THEATER
on West Broadway

It is thick here, the rise and fall of sidewalks,
fruit lounging in the space where we walk,
apples, oranges, melons, bananas, lights
from Christmas marking spots where clerks
gaze over the piles to catch hands slipping food
into pockets in one smooth swipe, and the moon
the accomplice, lending a shadow where no one
expects the moon to come to the aid of thieves.

Once friends made me laugh at the word
jur-is-dic-tion—sliding it until it slipped, pulling
it like a banana to be elongated until it is squishy,
and the other word we mined with word games—
e-lon-gat-ed—wondering why the n_g space had to be
separated—why the gate had to have its hinge taken
away, the "e" pushed to the "d" to finish things
in the thin elegance of length, like the trains
turning into streams of sucking air beneath us.

We go back into the sound of the bellowing
made when dumpsters are filled with the junk
of taking apart lives inside these old apartments
on the west side, gutted is the word, as if guts
can walk the space from old New York to this,
as if the oldness was greatness, and who is to say
it was not Rose McClendon teaching a young
Ruby Dee the blessing of what it is for actors to eat
when nothing happens, the stage dull and dumb.

A sign in front of me says—*absolutely no laptops*—
so I use the phone that does laptop work but fits itself
into my hand, a prompter's box, heavy and squat.
There is that word, squat. Squat will not be squished
into. Only words waiting to jump into a life
are fit for scripts, the actors, our great silence.

INOSCULATION, AN ODE TO WALT WHITMAN

It is early afternoon and I take the PATCO train
over Ben Franklin Bridge, the Campbell's plant
near the shell of the house you bought with what
was left of time and circumstance, a short walk
from the Delaware, the river Washington crossed
with his foot on the edge of the boat, on softness
of throats too dark to speak against this democracy
that can forget when left to forget, the smokestacks
of places that turned wheels and chemicals and steel
bolts riveted to girders of these bridges, the train
a silent steel snake with corpuscular dreams
like the dream of this world of pursuing markets
of happiness. I am lost to the world of my neighbors
when I take this ride over to professorship, a giant
Snickers bar hidden in the pocket of one of my
only two sport coats, riding over to the office
with the same numbers as Sethe's house in *Beloved*,
as if I walk out of the river fully suited and tied
to be the nightmare demanding love from rooms
low on it, demanding that shadowy spaces will
take an invested belief in me, will grow, ripen
into an ending of all suspicion of my abilities,
so I can sit in these meetings we have in your house,
some memorial to you, the house empty of the mess
that was your imprimatur, stacks of papers everywhere,
an assemblage greater than any Merz Schwitters
was ever able to call a work of art, the clutter
that is like the forced weaving that makes the stock

of soup that resists melting, our democratic dream,
as some squeak in the voice questions the possessive—
—*when did any of us ever utterly agree to "you?"*—
while at the bottom of this bridge that I rode to Philly
in a car with Gwendolyn Brooks I now go
underground to where my roots reveal tentacles
of my own doubt cast in me by those who love me.

III

A SOUTH CAROLINA
STATE OF NATION MIND

after Jay-Z

Mosquitoes drove whites upland to count
money Black overseers made, mosquitoes
made the air grow whelps on skin unused to what
makes money, the sun boiling Charleston Harbor,
boats chugging through the marsh with rice,
mosquitoes, not Blacks and their congresses
of prayer, disease like the riots in the land,
the second Civil War when Brown's decisions
set free Middle Passage ghosts, free so Blacks
could own corners, drive whites to the hills,
suburbs choking with Nigerian petroleum,
back to Africa again for investment capital,
triangles of oil, dope, experimental drugs,
mosquitoes drove whites upland to count
votes when the cities turned Black and Black
mayors won the empty space of abandoned
plantations, mosquitoes, insects with some grand
connection to God, wings pulled apart by children
who voted the first Black man to oversee a country
tearing its own guts apart to escape history.

MIDNIGHT AIR IN LOUISVILLE

for Breonna Taylor

Dear Breonna,
How many times, I ask,
      how many times
have I chased the thought
          of writing to you,
of catching the poem where
          it cannot leave,
of knocking open the door to a grief
      we all hold, our hearts
full of questions.
        We leave our houses to work,
to look for what we need to live,
         or what we need
      to make the pain go away,
and your voice rises:
      "Oh hell to the no,
no he didn't,
      Satan get behind me,
whatever, whatever
      the hell you think you are."

I imagine that in leaving
all of us you said:
      "I am done
I am let out into the world,
      breath I took in from it
breath that I give back in love."

May I see you in flight
filling the space
        beyond clouds and stars
where there is no need
        of sun or moon, where
a grand city lives
        in prophecies beaten
by the wheels of history
where you are not invisible
        to ancestors who saw
these long roads down through time
to this one night in Louisville.

        Bright Angel,
Luminescence, Woman Who Saved Lives
in Emergency Rooms,
                Invocation of Heaven's Law,
Living Song Riding
                the Eternal Dawn.

These titles I summon from license
given by Eternal Mysteries to hold you.
Fly now, in the woven air of the saints.

THIS CIVIL WAR YET UNRESOLVED

at Antietam

The river Ganges is on *NPR* all upside the fence
running past the bumper of the car I have forgotten,
rough rails laid in Xs in places, stiff, stoic,
the river on the other side of the world where souls
remember instead of forgetting, folk washing
lives like dirty clothes, while I creep around corners
where the rifles and the screaming songs of the dead
lie in the grass to be awakened again. Some Southern
way sings in me, *this is the ground I know.*

For a soldier there is a last day written in a diary
we learn in training, one thing at a time, assemble,
disassemble, take the carriage apart in fifteen
seconds, apply a steady hand to the wound when
packs are too far away, hold the blood when it wants
to go, sing the prayer song your mother taught you
when she was about to make the journey cross
the river. Stonewall Jackson said, *Let us lie
up under the tree for awhile and stop aching.*

I got a mind to get out of the car and walk all over
this killing field, but the air conditioner is like
Jack Daniels with Coke in the evenings, on a porch,
letting the air slide across the fields, a porch
like the one I see now, my barefoot and kind uncle
sleeping off the life of sharecroppers' sons, the wealth
of white sand caking around their ankles spotted
with rain, and I know the justice of these fields.
The way corn raises its throat to a God who went
somewhere and sat down to rest his nerves.

WHEN THE SLAVERS DIED AT SEA

The dread came over the edge of the deep
with the lightening of the sky, the yellow peek
into time, and when the ship came without

him, the dread became the terror of having
a heart's skin peeled back from love the way
columns and clumps of people were tucked

away in the ships, out in the midst of waters,
history's maker in a black lace dress tucking
them by the two or three hundred onto shelves,

touching them with some mystic caretaking
when their heads rolled with the whim of oceans,
tapping the tiny Black feet of children to wake

their hearts when it seemed they were sliding
off, the way the bodies of sailor husbands hit
the water in angles, then plunked down to look

for the bottom of things, where stories end
themselves on other sides of the eyes of fish
with gel lips. There is this hardness to life.

BACK SPIN OF HOPE

for Tupac Shakur

Here at the flat cup and empty bubble gum wrapper
    Whatup with Baby Drake?
        No hope in baseball, no hope in baseball
            Spare ribs $1, pork chops free
    That's dope, that's dope, back spins and rims
        Hook a brother up?

Here at the flat cup and empty bubble gum wrapper
    Whatup with Cheese?
        No hope in baseball, no hope in baseball
            Spare ribs $1, pork chops free
    That's dope, that's dope, back spins and rims
        Hook a brother up?

Here at the flat cup and empty bubble gum wrapper
    Whatup with Muslimah?
        Listen lil brother, the hoop, the hoop . . .
            Spare ribs $1, pork chops free
    That's dope, that's dope, back spins and rims
        Hook a sister up?

Here at the flat cup and empty bubble gum wrapper
    Whatup with you, G?
        Wade, wade in the water, swim, child!
            Spare ribs $1, pork chops free
    That's dope, that's dope, back spins and rims
        Hook a sister up?

Here at the flat cup and empty bubble gum wrapper
　　Whatup with Miss BayBay?
　　　　Hey caine copper, I got the girl . . .
　　　　　　　Fried fish sandwich $1, greens free
　　That's dope, that's dope, back spins and rims
　　　　Don't get on my bad side

Here at the flat cup and empty bubble gum wrapper
　　Whatup, Smooth?
　　　　No hope in baseball, no hope in baseball
　　　　　　Fried fish sandwich $1, greens free
　　That's dope, that's dope, back spins and rims
　　　　Gimme some dap!

Here at the flat cup and empty bubble gum wrapper
　　Whatup Peaches?
　　　　Shine, shine, who got the wine?
　　　　　　Fried fish sandwich $1, greens free
　　That's dope, that's dope, back spins and rims
　　　　Hook a sister up?

Here at the flat cup and empty bubble gum wrapper
　　Whatup with Pookie?
　　　　Wade, wade in the water, swim, child!
　　　　　　One pig foot 50 cents, two for a dollar
　　That's dope, that's dope, back spins and rims
　　　　Gimme some dap!

Here at the flat cup and empty bubble gum wrapper
  Where Sharanda go at?
    No hope in baseball, no hope in baseball
        One pig foot 50 cents, two for a dollar
   That's dope, that's dope, back spins and rims
      Handle your business, son

Here at the flat cup and empty bubble gum wrapper
  Where Conscience go at?
    Eyeballs, roll 'em cause you can't shoot 'em
        Corn pudding $2 a pound tonite
   That's dope, that's dope, back spins and rims
      Dat's tight, dat's tight, crack it!

Here at the flat cup and empty bubble gum wrapper
  Where DayDay go at?
    Shootin hoops, shootin dope, shootin . . .
        Corn pudding $2 a pound tonite
   That's dope, that's dope, back spins and rims
      Dat's tight, dat's tight, crack it!

Here at the flat cup and empty bubble gum wrapper
  Whatup with Poo Man?
    No hope in baseball, no hope in baseball
        10 fried chicken wings for $3
   That's dope, that's dope, back spins and rims
      Don't get on my bad side . . .

Here at the flat cup and empty bubble gum wrapper
    Whatup with Preach?
        Eyeballs, roll em cause you can't shoot em
            10 fried chicken wings for $3
    That's dope, that's dope, back spins and rims
        Don't get on my bad side . . .

Here at the flat cup and empty bubble gum wrapper
    Where Daddy 3T go at?
        Shootin hoops, shootin dope, shootin . . .
            10 fried chicken wings for $3
    That's dope, that's dope, back spins and rims
        You ain't got to steal to keep it real . . .

Here at the flat cup and empty bubble gum wrapper
    Where Big Daddy go at?
        No hope in baseball, no hope in baseball
            10 fried chicken wings for $3
    That's dope, that's dope, back spins and rims
        You ain't got to steal to keep it real

Here at the flat cup and empty bubble gum wrapper
    Where Pookie go with Sharanda?
        No hope in baseball, no hope in baseball
            2 bowls of gumbo for a dollar
    That's dope, that's dope, back spins and rims
        Poppop sez *study long, study wrong* . . .

Here at the flat cup and empty bubble gum wrapper
    Where Pookie go at with Sharanda?
        Shine, shine, who got the wine?
                2 bowls of gumbo for a dollar
   That's dope, that's dope, back spins and rims
        Dat's tight, dat's tight, crack it!

Here at the flat cup and empty bubble gum wrapper
    Where Chantay at?
        No hope in baseball, no hope in baseball
                Who made this gumbo? Hey!
   That's dope, that's dope, back spins and rims
        Slide it on over here to me . . .

Here at the flat cup and empty bubble gum wrapper
    Is that Chantay with Pookie?
        Little Pete shootin some hoops today, boy . . .
                Frozen Kool-Aid popsicles 25 cents
   That's dope, that's dope, back spins and rims
        Slide it on over here to me . . .

Here at the flat cup and empty bubble gum wrapper
    What Chantay and Pookie doing?
        No hope in baseball, no hope in baseball
                Catsup sandwich 25 cents, air for free
   That's dope, that's dope, back spins and rims
        Kick it, kick it . . .

Here at the flat cup and empty bubble gum wrapper
        Where Chantay's mama go at?
            Handle your business, son . . .
                        Catsup sandwich 25 cents, air for free
        That's dope, that's dope, back spins and rims
                    Tight! Tight! Swing, swing, swing . . .
                    & don't mean a thing . . .

WHEN I THINK OF VIETNAM

Thinking of what is new, how nothing gets
beyond being already done, I stare at a decimated
apple seed, some unnamed rascal having made off
with the real fruit, my last hope for a spring
that is real, not the juggernaut of artificial corn.

I am perplexed, thinking perplexity is the door
to writing something new, a brave metaphor
or the last teenage dream I had in East Baltimore
before the naive wish to be thought worthwhile
by the grand machine, to become a soldier.

Then comes the sober sense of dogs roaming
streets where there is only a blank starvation,
and the awful stench of having eaten the planet
where we live all reminds me this poem must resist
all things that kill, things that add to war's breath.

The life that smothers and gluts us makes it tough
to see how love grows through a bitter humility,
the barely audible whisper of people too wise
to believe the lies we Americans tell ourselves
about who Americans are and what belongs to us.

SACRED

for Dr. Martin Luther King, Jr.

1—Moratorium to end the War in Vietnam

In a year after your leaving, we climbed
trees in the mall to hear your widow speak
to the silence you left beside her at night, the trick
of moonlight in the bedroom window pasting
her tears to cotton, we climbed up adolescent
and full, dumb to the bells that toll on the other side
of Providence, the jeeps and tanks protecting our
white houses, so long and deep the groaning wish
of pastors in Southern dust and wooden churches
with no conditioned air, only the spirituals, gospels
of life and death, howling in the woods, blood
crawling up the measures of a raw, open flesh,
the registers of souls making the blues, the jazz.

We climbed into the deadness of trees gone bare
to prepare for Washington's winter, Jefferson sculpted
on the other end in his stoniness, his eyes on the nation,
on us in these perches where we heard the whirl of some
near half million of us protesting the war we later
would go to—a jungle, heat, fire, napalm, monsoons
like the endless melting of envy, the surprise
of women and children tossing bombs at us after
smiling, and who teaches us to smile but innocence
and suffering, the frailty of age, gone as we are
after youth, after immortality, this war we could not see
but would prepare to live, later some of us in trees
training to shoot people who do not know where

we are, how we breathe, why we shoot to take life
away, the way piety and sanctity guarantee death.

2—Many thousands gone . . .

Maybe creation came as God cried, the tears
the violent origin of ego, the doubling, two,
four, eight–sixty-four, software and apocalypse,
our false divinity, so that death is the oneness,
three, five, seven, numbers knowing themselves
as one, life blossoming to thinness, invisibility,
away from the balcony, the rifle cracking the peace
of gazing out on the day with your plans, then the
lifting back into the place where there is nothing,
where oneness relieves itself of thinking.

In the midst of one and two, there is the dream you
dreamed of the end of perfection, how the sacred
wisdom is realizing we cannot fix anything, not
even our eyes on the first moments of a morning,
the cakewalk of wasp to whip-poor-will, the bliss
of an old blind dog finding his way to his food, the
Southern way of studying a soul, an epiphany
Martin Luther could not invoke with his prayers,
enraged by the Ballet of Chestnuts and Tetzel
with his indulgences, enraged into a pious madness,
a new culling of the imperfect away from us,
wishing death on Abraham and Sarah's children—
you saw this, too, pulling away from Earth from

the doubling, one for the moon, one for the sun,
your heart and mind now one flying away,
over everything we know, connecting masses,
stars and galaxies now the one light that knows
this world is mist and fog, a simple longing.

TO MALCOLM X ON HIS SECOND COMING

Malcolm X, alias El Hajj Malik El Shabazz,
alias Malcolm Little, alias Detroit Red—

                                 Deceased!

The coffin breaks, fingers wriggle through clay,
touch the light. A chiseled face comes full with flesh,
eyes roaming the landscape of his own prophecy.
Negroes in their Infinitis, Benzes, and BMWs,
chains of gold around their necks, fifty tons of gold
for teeth, sneakers handmade in the glass pavilions
of murderers. Hip hop stirring the empty souls.
Up from this tomb in our lost hopes, he stands
and prays into Allah's outstretched hands for mercy.

                    This is why he came back:
            on a plantation porch, Lil Missy
            plays with Liza, offering her lemonade.
            "Liza, tell me again about them runaways
            you turned in, them bad bucks daddy
            hanged and cut up, lovely little Liza Mae,
            brown eyes, brown eyes."

At five o'clock in the morning in Baltimore,
in Philadelphia, in New York, in Newark, in Chicago,
the fresh morning water of showers falls, and
the followers of Elijah utter their morning prayers.
Allah the Beneficent, Allah the Merciful,
All praises to Allah, and the Nation of Islam,

Hope of the Resurrection of the So-Called Negro,
comes to life, the life before the death of the Master.

> "Liza, where your mind, chile?
> me and the other boys had plans
> for bein free and comin back for y'all.
> my mama raised you from a little nothin,
> and you turned us in. Now we rottin
> in some place with no name, cut up
> like dog meat. Liza, where your mind?"

Malcolm walks in Harlem along the broken streets,
gathering mystified eyes. In Sylvia's he pokes his head in
and asks what food there is for the soul. Some woman
says, "You look just like Malcolm X. You shoulda been
in that movie that boy Spike Lee made." And she goes on
cutting up custard pies and singing a gospel song she wrote.
Malcolm goes over to St. Nicholas Avenue, looks down
on the city. Afternoon shadows begin to fall like
the difficult questions of his father. Malcolm mourns
his mother, the abyss she fell into and could not escape,
the abyss of his genius. In a glimmer an angel settles
on his shoulder, as small as a pin but with a voice like
a choir singing. "No more grief, blessed son, no more grief."
Malcolm falls to the pavement, sobbing for Elijah.

> Lil Missy sits in her bedroom chair,
> sewing eyes on her doll, singing.
> Liza listens to night sounds, afraid

of darkening the door to tomorrow.
Lil Missy says, "Liza, come round here
and rub my feet befo you go to
my daddy's room."

In the Audubon ballroom the night he was killed,
Malcolm X saw his assassins rise amid a host of spirits
battling for his life. Demons and angels filled the space,
battling for his soft head, as his eyes took Allah's kiss.
His murder was a rupture in the world of the spirit,
the demons rushing desperately to name their position
in the African heart, where the angels fought to defend
God's voice uttering His own holy name, Allah.
Malcolm's head hit the stage like a giant stone
from Zimbabwe landing on Earth. His mind
took on its silence while his spirit was filled with song.
"Oh, blessed son, come unto me. Oh, blessed son."

In front of the Schomburg, Malcolm rises
above the city, his mind covering all of Harlem,
while he issues the manifesto:

On self-defense:
strike me, and I will strike you back
On freedom:
freedom is a fire waiting to come
On the future:
no profit will come from destruction

On the Nation of Islam:
the saved are still saving

Caravans form in the streets, unloading
the unconscious souls. The open eyes of the living dead
stare from windows and shops at this voice
that is in every doorway, this body that is the landscape,
as if the city is now flesh. In one moment he is there,
and then he is gone, letting their bodies go softly
back into time. Negroes wonder what has been
among them and is now gone. Malcolm sits on steps
on Convent Avenue, again just another man.
An old woman pulling a cart comes to him, touches
his head, and both of them vanish into Allah's wish.

The wise among us chant the filling of our life with life,
take this fragment of a gift from heaven and anoint
the heads of the young, who are our promise to live—

Teach, Master, teach. Teach, Master, teach.
Teach, Master, teach. Wa Alaikum Salaam.

EPHEMERA

Each morning I sit in silence, time slides, changes
in my heart, a moss-covered cavern where its fire
wakes me to a camaraderie of light, my wife waking

upstairs to walk to her window to pray, to gaze
outward at the pasture where Wappinger people eyed
white men making laws to own people and the land.

Art rules this old house, its rough rafters set in earth
as the colony became a state, and Poughkeepsie forgot
its own wonder, a gathering of reeds on banks of a river

Hudson believed would take him to China, his breath
unnoticed these days by the hummingbirds that visit
our door, sounds of their wings like my fingers tapping

my mother's empty Tupperware bowl, with cake batter
a thin film she let me lick only when I was good, the taste
something I let leave as I sit, waiting to be aware, woke

as some say. I imagine the sun, its fire, its electricity,
waiting for us when we have lived all we can live, hoped
all we can hope, some of us snatched away by the virus,

corona wrath of a world disturbed. Surprised as we
are by nature's decisions, we refuse to surrender,
to let go of what kills us when we try to control all

of what we cannot see. Our house is now inside me.
It is me, I am it, my bowels and spine its forgotten
birth, my thinning skeleton now its heavy rafters,

my emptiness its emptiness, my fullness its fullness,
or ideas of the breath, our two minds held still by
the fastening of it all, hook and joint, sinew and bone.

GOD IS

for Camille and Jim

inside the most quiet and still moments in your studio at night, the suggestion of
 a song

in the ticklish part of taking a shower and feeling utterly like the child of your
 mama

the most unspoken regret you share with no one but know is known by your art

a way the floor creaks when you think this man who is your husband is thinking

the way a wish seems to be in the night sky when you stare long enough at the
 lights

breakfast at the table with the black cat knowing everything you have forgotten

what you dream of youth and what a woman can do to make a man weep

touch and what touch is, your fingers to paper, the nakedness of your feet to
 the earth

a belly beautiful grasp on what laughter lies inside realities like being "totally
 niggerish"

the real meaning of 在我的裡面有一個複雜的事情 when you forget it's in
 Chinese

what LA was when you were nine years old and there was another kind of
 negro in America

the sound of wind in Egypt at night when you are beyond time and in the
arms of secrets

wishes and wherefores and what lies in the blank stares of a South Carolina
sweet potato pie

seamstresses of the soul who spin their thread in memories of rent parties
on <u>11th street</u>

that Black man who liked to call you "Hat" and the mystery of what negroes
do to English

collard greens and biscuits and the way the city feels when you leave all the
cities you know

imagination or just what it is to lie down for weeks in chains in the bottom of a
boat called Jesus

Or all art and what that needs to be in a world so fucked up it is beautiful beyond
all dreams